HOWARD WHITE

Howard White is the founder and president of
Harbour Publishing, editor of *Raincoast Chronicles,*
and owner of a heavy construction company in
Pender Harbour, B.C. He was born in Abbotsford
in 1945 and spent his early days in logging camps up
and down the west coast. In 1976 he won the
Eaton's B.C. Book Award for *Raincoast Chronicles:
First Five.* He is twice winner of Canadian Media
Club Awards for Best Magazine Feature. He has
published in *Sound Heritage, Poetry Canada Review,
Macleans, Event, The Vancouver Sun, The Vancouver
Province, Energy File, B.C. Outdoors, Pacific Yachting*
and *Books In Canada.* Some of the poems in this
book first appeared in the work anthologies *A
Government Job at Last* and *Going for Coffee.* Howard
White is a member of the International Union of
Operating Engineers. He lives in Pender Harbour
and works as Solid Waste Supervisor of the Sanitary
Disposal Unit.

The Men
There Were Then

Howard White

Arsenal Editions
Vancouver

THEM MEN THERE WERE THEN
COPYRIGHT © 1983 HOWARD WHITE

ARSENAL EDITIONS
Box 3868 MPO, Vancouver BC Canada V6B 3Z3
A Division of Arsenal Pulp Press Book Publishers Ltd.

TYPESETTING: *Baseline Publication Trades Co-op.*

PRINTING: *First Folio Printing Co. Ltd.*

COVER: *Bryan Wert & David Robinson*

CANADIAN CATALOGUING IN PUBLICATION DATA
White, Howard
    The men there were then
Poems.
ISBN 0-88978-109-5 (BOUND).
ISBN 0-88978-097-8 (PBK.)
I. Title.
PS8595.H57M4   C811'.54   C83-091077-8
PR9199.3.W49M4

ACKNOWLEDGEMENTS
Some of these poems have been previously published in *Sound Heritage,
Poetry Canada Review, Event, A Government Job at Last, Going for Coffee,* and
3¢ Pulp.

PRINTED AND BOUND IN CANADA

for Mary

THE MEN THERE WERE THEN

INTRODUCTION

If the truth be known I'm not much better at bulldozer driving than I am at being a poet, but I've always been able to turn a lot of heads with the combination.

One of my early memories is of being squeezed in beside my father on the driver's seat of his new D-8 cat as he flattened the maple grove behind our house on Nelson Island. These were awesome trees and we kids lived in their shadow, humble. We didn't love them but we didn't question them. They were cornerposts of God's creation, ancient as grandfather time—and the D-8 trashed them in minutes. Hunching down saucer-eyed beside my father that afternoon was one of those experiences like a severe earthquake that leaves one's faith in the ultimate solidity of things forever shaken. It was a shock, but it was exciting too, because this unthinkable force was guided by my father's hand and he was using it to make a clearing where my mother could grow a garden and we kids could play in the sun.

It was huddled another time beside my father, this time in his musty old easychair listening as he read "The Walrus and the Carpenter" the umpteenth time, by request, that I decided the other thing I wanted to do some day besides run my own bulldozer was to write my own book. It would be a poem about a tractor that heroically got carrots to grow right out of regular dirt, an amazing thought.

My operating career came along a lot easier than my writing one. By age eight I had my first machine—the dump winch for unloading trucks at my Dad's logging camp—and all through school I helped work the family sand and gravel business. I was the only kid in our area who, when he missed the schoolbus, came to class in a ten-yard tandem dump.

When I went to college I started following heavy construction in the summers, doing a lot of pretty things like bulldozing farms in the Revelstoke Valley so it could be flooded by some pointless Social Credit dam (I've since written a contrite poem.) After four years of that I was half a course short of my B.A. from U.B.C., which I've never bothered to make up because by then I'd earned the piece of paper that mattered — my operator's ticket from Local 115 of the I.U.O.E. Without that I might never have become Solid Waste Supervisor at the Pender Harbour Sanitary Disposal Unit. (I muck out the trash with a bucket loader and never find anything good.)

I'm rather pleased that this book, although it has no carrots that I can think of, does feature a number of tractors. I didn't realize until I started writing this introduction what a tidy little thread of consistency this ties around what I'd always assumed to be a completely formless existence. I'm a bit embarrassed that it's taken thirty-five years to bring off, but I shouldn't have to take all the blame for that. Some of the poems included here were written as long ago as the mid-sixties, but clashed so violently with the literary taste of that time that I spent the next decade convinced they were unpublishable. The way it was explained to me was that my subject matter, being mostly about people working, was too limited. I should have widened my terms of reference and abstracted my material into themes of greater intellectual significance, I was told. Today I find the same poems being held up as examples of what has come to be called industrial writing — and the present publisher wanted, at one point, to cut from the book anything that *didn't* deal with people working. I realize that this doesn't automatically discredit my earlier critics but it has taught me something I thought I already knew about following one's own path.

If I've had a formal concern in writing these poems it has been to explore the genius of common speech as I have heard it from the people I live and work among. The Accident Series probably represents the most direct manifestation of this concern. Every job I've ever been on I've seen the same thing happen: people sit down to talk and sooner or later they end up talking about accidents. The stories are usually offered as eyewitness accounts and told with such hair-raising detail you'd think they must be; but more often than not they're ones you've heard before with different victims in different places. I have long been intrigued by this phenomenon. I see it as an authentic legendary tradition flourishing right in the midst of modern industry, a species of oral literature that rivals the written variety in its refinement of effect.

I have been asked what made me decide to present a lot of this material in verse form. I will concede that it's a good question. The answer might be that the whole argument about what is and what isn't a poem has ceased to worry me very much. I like to think of what Ezra Pound, that oracle of poetic technique, said when he came to Thomas Hardy. Here was a writer who seemed oblivious to the demands of form, yet Pound had to admit that he loved his work. So he did a second take on all his prescriptions for good writing and added this proviso: "There will always be a place for the man who has a story to tell." I wouldn't want to be accused of comparing myself to Hardy, but I find comfort in Pound's excuse.

The makers of the great primitive legends, the authors of the great epics, the troubadors, the Elizabethan playwrights, didn't consider it beneath them to tell a story, but modern poetry does and this has made it the preserve of an incidental minority while the mass of people are abandoned to Warner Bros.

It doesn't have to be that way.

Accidents

LUNCHING ON MYTH

Perched on the log our
catskinner comrade left for the
purpose, wax paper and apples
precarious thermos bottles
exhaling white breath
at the chill day   our talk
starts variously, finds its way
always here: heads
"smashed like an egg"
arms pulled from their sockets
with a pop, the poor
greenhorn greasemonkey
who gets his skull shot full
of high-pressure grease

stories of ingenious death
details honed to a
murderous edge
to make you forget how
many times you heard
that one before

each teller in turn
a poet for the moment
truth set aside
as we pick among
the scrapyards of our days
like the sparrows at the shop
that make their nest
of rusty steel wool

weaving myth
of the only
deaths that are left

CORKY

I

It was at Nanoose in '42
had this little guy loading
        "Corky"
bouncy kind of a guy
natural clown
you'd hafta grin
just lookin at him—
whatever he was doin
it always looked like an act

he was up on the load swingin a log
pushin it straight
with both arms out
as it came down
landing cat snagged the line
log jumped at him
he sprang back straight
back like a cat
off the truck
knew where his browskid was
without lookin
just like a cat
landed on it perfect
but his corks didn't catch
—fulla bark—
slid down beside the skid
head went "crack"

someone said jeez
you can hear the echo
we all laughed

he was just sittin there
where he landed
legs out straight like a puppet
arms down and the longer he stayed
the more we laughed
four or five of us
standing there laughin
waiting
went on a bit
long
someone says, hey
you all right?

he was dead.
little spike knot
size of a two-inch nail
went through the back of his head

II

What struck them
was the deadweight flop
of his body, the ordinary
smacking noise on the dirt
of what a minute ago
was light of step,
giving them cheek —

for him too,
an event clothed
in the ordinary
slipping in under
his guard
the inevitability
evident
only at the last
breath before death

a familiar arrangement
of moments, the boom
swinging, the man standing
ready as so many times before.
The load not falling right,
again as often before,
the corrective push
leading him in — things
in themselves simple,
in combination deadly.

If only. At this point anything —
a passing bird to turn
his head, a shout if anyone
had been quick enough
to decode,
might have changed it.

Frame by frame in the watchers' minds
the moments replayed forever
looking for the seam

in his frozen forever
the jokemaking ordinariness
of his day slowing,
growing rich in detail
to that broken
open moment
cold wind blowing in

WRINGERS

George Weeks likes to tell about the time
him and his grampa saw the old lady
catch her hand in the gas-powered wringer
watched laughing as she went in
stamping and hollering to the armpit
then instead of hitting the release hit the reverse lever
all the way back out
stamping and hollering
except this time the roller
squeezed all the blood up ahead
bulging her forearm up like Popeye
blew the nails out of her fingers
then the old girl did have something

to holler about

Later saw his cousin catch a finger
in one of the big rollers
in the Crofton paper room
arm was gone in a flash
just this big 'pop'
of the shoulder letting go
see him sitting around the Inn
drinking his draught one-armed
saying the only thing he remembers
was that first little nip

on the fingertip

DEATH OF A FALLER

Uppit Englewood there one time
I was blowin whistles, scaler
busts out of the bush   hollers
get a stretcher — fallers bin burned

was cuttin upwards on a big leaning fir
gascap unscrewed   doused im down is front
then lit im up
just black goo from is ribs to is knees

all he seemed to be worried about was
he had to take a pee, passin out
and comin to all the way down
lemmee down keeps sayin

dont wanna piss on this new stretcher
sez to me I got a kid like you
do me a favour kid
stick my pecker over the side

thing was it was his works that was
burnt worst of all —
his knob was just a
black twist of ash

when we rolled him on the stretcher
it just fell off in the moss
where we left it
like nobody saw

what could you say
I was still trying to think
when I realized
he was dead

BABY FAT

I saw a log drop one time
and pop a man's head like a kelp bulb
blood doesn't bother me
but this one time
my eldest daughter she was
about so high then
used to give her the
greasegun
send her under the truck
to grease the throwout bearing
could do it standing up
thought it was great fun
but her hair was blonde and
soft like bullrush fluff
she'd come back right
black, jeez the wife
would scream

she tripped on a cut open
barrel I had for washing parts
tore a four-inch gash
in er leg   didn't bleed
at all
but this white babyfat
bushed out like popcorn
under the pressure like

she was going to turn right
inside out
the doctor just shoved it in with his thumb
and slapped on a bandage

but I damn near fainted

CAT TRACKS

Nothing I hate worsen cat tracks
just lookin at em
my back goes out
that's where I lost this finger
caught it between two pads
nipped it off
worst thing is they've got that great huge
spring in there
holden em tight
that you're always workin against
one got away on me once
damn near took the whole wall
right out of the damn shop
had an eight-foot wrench
to set em up
better now with those
hydraulic adjusters
just a grease nipple there
all you do is pop your greasegun on it
but those damn things are dangerous too
quart of grease in there
that big spring coiled up behind it
like a loaded cannon
saw a kid once
come n start unscrewin that nipple
thought it was
just another greasepoint
musta bin bent close over it
hard to get a wrench on

got it out to the last turn
nipple let fly like a shotgun slug
straight for the eye
he was watching it with
grease poked out like an iron rod
followed the nipple
a quart of grease is
just what the skull would hold
when we found him
looked perfectly alright
except for the one eye gone
and his mouth kinda popped open
like a red snapper
when you catch it down deep
something white
musta bin is brains

THE TOOTH

Did ten years at Crofton
    shift work
           almost had me
worked in the boiler room
with this old guy
    "Archie"
had more seniority than
anyone else in the mill
had a gold front tooth
all I remember now
of what he looked like
faces all the time covered
up with goggles and masks
bundled up in thick wool suits
hundred degrees in there already
but if the caustic
touched your skin it'd eat
right through to bone
great two-storey vats there
molten caustic soda
bubbling fuming and yellow
worse than any acid
catwalks around 'em
dropped a fourteen-inch
stilson into it once
got it back next shift
all ate into filaments

like alder lace
when old Archie
stumbled off the catwalk
all we got back
    was his tooth

I KILL MYSELF AND MAIM MYSELF

As often as I think to, as many ways
as I can arrange. I never miss
a chance, on top of a boom
to miss a handhold and plunge
five storeys onto blasted rock.
Beneath a building going up
I always cause a rigging wrench
or a piece of just-cut plate
to plunge jagged and sizzling
into my skull. Under trucks
draining hot oil I let them
roll over me harmlessly except for
one low-hanging bolt which catches
my shoulder and rolls me into a
dusty oily boneless ball.
I never see a set of rollers but
I offer my hand, my wrist, my
crunching elbow, shoulder jams
skin burns and pulls loose
horrible snapping as of bridge timbers
breaking and the arm is gone.
The moment I arrive in presence
of a new machine, I surrender myself.
I watch its bearings strain and
break as the soles of my shoes
disappear and I come out below,
gear tracks in pink froth, foreman
cursing my stupidity, men wondering
who'll get number seven now.

Tail-swings have scissored my head off
so many times. And snapping cables
like bullwhips after my balls.
I torment myself alive.
I kill and maim myself and daily pray
to confine disaster to the mind.

THE MEN THERE WERE THEN

It sounds like something that's been
said before too many times
but I want you to know
I mean it, now, when I say
there are no men around today
like the men there were then.
You see those enormous tree stumps
with the notches in, and you don't think.
Those were big trees.
There are no trees like that today.
We think today what we do with machines
is hard work, but our trees are tiny
and they did it all by hand.
They did it all standing on springy, narrow
boards, stuck twelve feet up above the ground
sometimes canyons below them
swinging their axes into that big wood.
To move along they'd give a hop with one toe
held under the springboard, to swing it.
Then they'd stick the axe in the wood
and stoop to reach their saws, I never
heard of one who fell.
But one time one man when he
turned to reach for his saw,
he brushed that razor sharp axe
and it slit his middle
right along the belt line for about eight inches.
It didn't bleed so much but

his intestines came looping down like bunting.
When we came with the stretcher this man
was under the cut crouched on his knees
delicately holding up these gut loops
one by one splashing sawdust off 'em
with water from his waterbag.
There are no men like that
around today.

WHAT A WAY TO GO

He was haywire, terrible haywire,
old Farraro.
And that was what did him in.
They were tearing down a house.
Some free deal old Farraro'd got in on,
halfway up Black Mountain
and as usual they had a
terrible old truck that just barely ran.
They got this truck up there,
and I suppose they put a huge load on
which was bad enough right there,
but the worst thing was,
they had no ropes to tie the load down.
They would never think of a thing like that
beforehand, and apparently there was
none around, up on this mountain.
So the old man he took one boy
and sat out back, boy on the lumber
to weigh it down, and him up
on a big stack of naily plywood.
Well the brakes of course went,
and halfway down away they go.
Gino was the one at the wheel,
and by jesus now if he didn't
hold er on the road all the way down—
it musta gone a hundred miles an hour.
The kid and all the shiplap,
which was on the tail,
went off at the first bump, and after

34

they got all the rusty nails out of im
he was okay. But the old man,
he hung on. You can just see im
sittin' up there like a cowboy on a brahma bull
trying to save his plywood pile.
Still, there wasn't much else to do.
The kid saw it all, said he was
doing okay till just about the
bottom of the hill, when finally
the wind got under the edge and up he went
like a sultan on a magic carpet
soaring on this naily sheet of plywood
hundrit miles an hour,
right out over the rockslide.
He went down a thousand feet.
But just think of it eh, sittin' there
both eyes open watchin'
the end of er fly up in your face
couldn't even get a hand free
to cross himself—

HARDHAT DIVER

You always hear about the guy who was
diving on a wreck by that big hole
up in the Portland Canal

old style diving suit
with the round helmet
just like a fishbowl

the wreck shifted
hauled him over the edge
and down a hundred fathoms

guy on the hoist just paid out line
till it stopped and jiggled it free
when they got him back

1950's LSD

Was he drunk? It was the next day.
Was green for go,
or red for stop?
TURN! she said,
my god, you almost didn't turn!

losing his mind at the strange party
people waved the next day
and smiled broadly — that
the price of friendship
in this town, simply get
some shit on you too

Now you go right home and
take a shower and don't
plunk any poles on the way.
She looked like a robin at him.
Don't let it get ahold of you
like that. You're letting it.
OK! he said

sat up fierce looking
rammed the gearshift in
saluted, took off
straight across the school grass
hundreds of faces at the windows
principal almost too astounded
to remember the police

I must keep the red needle
on the little side of fifty
he said to himself aloud
but when bad shit boiled up
he stamped it out with his foot
breathed deep wind roared
in his ears

his head the cop said when
she was crying and couldn't
hear, was right inside
the speedometer, wires in his eyes
looked funny as hell

THE HAIR

Watcha lookin' at, kid? he said
jaggedly, waving the stump
of his arm in my face
Eh? Nothin'? I thought I noticed
you was starin' at somethin'

And the truth is I really wasn't
it barely caught my eye but
that was enough to catch him
The least you can do is
siddown have a beer—

The fact there was no way out
making it no easier to take,
the stump standing between us
blocking thought
Go ahead, ask me, he says

that's what you want ain't it?
myself not so sure
not wanting any of this
kinda hoping to find that
new girl who works in the cookhouse

It was a hair done this to me,
he said. A hair just this long.
You think I'm shittin' ya, eh?
You think I got no brains
because I got no arm, I know—

deny it like hell but what
you guys forget is I was just the same
one time and would be still—
he fumbled his beer this fury
now his only pleasure

People say it was the rollers
but I worked around them rollers
for eighteen months
and they never took it then.
It wasn't the rollers.

I don't know if you ever worked
in a place where nothing ever happens
except the same thing about
seven thousand times a day.
It's only the danger keeps you alive

and even that you gotta work at.
Small things get big.
That was the week Joe told that
good joke, you'd say.
This day

it was one a them curly hairs in
your nose starts tickling,
makin' ya sneeze, you know?
I picked it a bit, rubbed it
till it got sore but you know

I kinda didn't want to get it
because it was something to do.
All I remember about the day
is that hair. I musta done

all the usual set-up 'n start-up,
changed two rolls they tell me,
oiled all 200 oil holes
but the only thing I can remember
is that hair.

And then the nip of the finger
flesh all squeezing up
towards my shoulder and bursting
rollers red, bits a me
whipping around

nurses laughed, said when I was under
all I could talk about was this
hair, wanted 'em to operate
on this hair in my nose
like it was the only thing that mattered

POWDER

The old fuse-type blasting caps
you could set off with a loud curse
they gave you these special little
plastic pliers to crimp them on with
but I always did it with my teeth
doesn't bother me longs I can see it—
why I say never hide an explosive—
old man used to squirrel
his caps away in little drawers,
find 'em years later, digging around
looking for something

had a lot of missing fingers

or old powder. I won't go near it.
You never know where it is
the nitro leaks out of the sticks
gets old and ornery
you never know where it is
it might be in the ground
beside the box, blow you up
just walking by. That's why
they put that brown wax paper
in the boxes, to catch the nitro—

used to work for a gyppo, Jim Ross,
up Frederick's Arm, decided he could
be his own powderman

saw him in the Austin a couple
years ago, you never seen a man
so busted up and still alive
friends had to pack him around—

he'd been tryin to use up an old
case of stumping powder, opened 'er
up real careful, took out the top row
of sticks and they wouldn't blow.
Worked his way down, row after row,
none of it would blow. Went back,
the box was empty. So, what
happened? I said. He said,

I tried to pick up the paper.

SHAFTS

Look so innocent neatly spinning away
soundless, conccaling their viciousness
in bright-metal symmetry
waiting for that
                  dangling shoelace
                  unbuttoned cuff
to set their mayhem loose
hungry for human limbs

Never forget old Slim Finlay
rotten-tempered welding mechanic
at Pioneer for years
wore the same pair of coveralls
all the time I was there
black like plastic
caught a dangling cuff and boom
he's standing there in nothing
but pink silk underpants

Worst on boats
guys out there all alone working
in and around spinning gurdy drives
on slimy, pitching decks
humming propeller shafts in rolling fishy holds
was in at Alert Bay when that guy on the Polar III
lost his old lone wolf troller
bent it wrong way around the tailshaft
tore off at the knee
did it up in a bedsheet tourniquet

ran in five hours   nosed into the dock
leaned on his whistle till people came
made us ice the fish wash the decks
turn off the fuel tanks lock everything
refused to stay in the hospital
too many goddamn wimmin
pawing at him all the time, he said
crawled around his boat in a padded bandage
tinkering and painting till the doctors
let him go back out fishing
grumbling like the whole episode was some
inexcusable invasion of his privacy

THE THIRD STIFF

Far as getting busted up goes it's safer on a boat
than most shore jobs   safest job there is
if you don't count drowning
Gillnetters especially
out on deck for a beer piss
boat leans one way
you lean the other—
kersplash.
Or reaching out over the rollers
to shake a log out of the web.
They find your boat idling up against a bluff
the next day, tow it into the float
nobody will tie up next to it.
One year up in Rivers Inlet
three guys went over in one week.

What happens then, they turn up a few days later
in other guys' nets. Guy'd see this lump coming up
and think it was a seal till it falls on deck
and an arm flops out to signal
shit-your-drawers time.
Two of these corpses showed up on schedule
but the third one kept us guessing for a while.
Fishermen are a spooky lot to begin with
and you have to have done it to know just how eerie
it gets out there in the middle of the night
all by yourself leaning over the stern   .
wondering just what sort of a ghastly item

the murk is going to puke up at you next
everybody in the inlet was just quaking in their gumboots
every time they saw something that wasn't a fish
come into the light figuring for sure
they'd snagged the third stiff

Sonny Iverson said this night he got so bad
he had to go knock back half a twenty-sixer
before he could get the rest of his net in
leaning over the stern to pull kelp out of the rudderpost
thinking what a damn fool he was to get so spooked
the whisky took his balance and plop
he's in the soup   his faithful boat
gliding serenely away into the night
and all he can think about is that damn stiff—
'now I'm in here with that sonofabitch!'
he's afraid to paddle, certain when he reaches out
he'll touch it and once when he brushes a chunk
he finds himself screaming like he's being murdered.
Then he hears something.
A kind of a faint swishing noise.
Swish, swish, swish—
He listens real careful and reaches around a bit.

There, right under his nose, is a moving line of corks.
Somebody is picking their net past him and all he has to do
is grab on and wait to be saved.
This works fine until he comes up to the other boat
and finds he's all tangled up in the net
and before he can say anything he's up over the rollers

crashes head first on the deck and knocks himself silly.
Of course the other fisherman just cuts loose
swearing and cursing all the foul luck in the world
figuring it's the missing stiff he's hooked onto
until Sonny starts coming to and moaning a bit
then the poor guy runs howling the length of the boat
bars himself into the house
cursing God and praying to be saved at the same time
it takes Sonny fifteen minutes to calm him down enough
to go get his boat

NET MEN

Gillnet drums can give a guy a scare
always leaning over them as they turn
flipping out fish, clearing tangles
guys would catch their hands in the spooling web
get wound up in their own net.
They invented a foot control that stops everything
as soon as your weight goes off it
but every so often some bright-eye comes along
rigs up a drum in his speedboat
with some haywire damned hand-control
kid did it up off Cape Caution one year
other boats heard him screaming
came over while he was still going around
what a mess   web cut into him
some places three inches deep
terrific pressure on that stretchy nylon
as it piles on that drum
broke every bone in his body
even his little toe
everything squished out of him
all mashed together with the fish
he'd had in his net
decided to leave him where he was
run the boat into Hardy Bay
let the doctors do what they want
but he died before they got very far
thing was fishing was real poor all week
but this guy had filled his net
heard them on the radio

'Stupid bastard musta had 500 anyway—'
had to line up

to get his spot

THOSE BLOODY FISHERMEN

Those bloody fishermen you know
they're not even human
not during fishing season
you know old Scotch John
take a look at
that man's hands if you ever
get the chance
left or right I forget,
one of 'ems got a hole
right through it
'e was running 'is lines out one time
feeling the fathom markers
with the flat of 'is hand, it was
the old bronze type of line, and a loose strand speared 'im
clean through the fingers
threaded 'em tight together
yanked 'im overboard
but 'e hit the gurdy clutch
goin' by   climbed back in
one-handed   cut the fingers apart
with sidecutters
each one separately
went on fishing
holes started stinkin' n goin' green
so he soaked 'em in the bleach bucket
he had there for his spoons
poked out the gunk with a broomstraw, holes got so big
'e could see through 'em
white furry stuff lining 'em

still he couldn't miss any fishing
holes closed up eventually
went bluish black   saw a doctor
end of the season, said
didn't that hurt?
Hurt? he sez, yeah by God it hurt
like a son of a bitch
passed our right there
in the doctor's chair
said later that was the
first time 'e stopped to think about it
and it hit 'im all at once

PUG HAYDEN

Pug Hayden had been in the pro ring for years
but he wasn't the defensive type of fighter.
He could hit like a holstein bull
but when it came to stopping a punch
often as not he stopped it with his head.
It left him with some loose wires.

Pug worked on the second shift.
The super was a guy named Steeves.
Every time Steeves run into Pug he'd throw up his dukes,
yell, "Come on Killer," and have a big laugh.
It wasn't so funny to the rest of us
but Steeves was a super
and I guess he figured that made it alright
for him to be laughing when nobody else was laughing.
The only one who'd laugh for him was Pug
because Pug was good natured as a Newfoundland pup.

One day Steeves come busting around a corner and run slam into Pug.
Steeves jumped back and squared off as usual
but it happened a bit too quick for Pug.
He drove the guy so hard it took six teeth out.
Next thing he was down on his knees
picking up teeth, begging Steeves to forgive him,
Steeves was meowing, "Sheeziss Chris' Bug, I wash shush kidding ya—"

I know there isn't much chance of it
but I always like to think Pug did that one accidentally

on purpose.

THESE HERE POETS

Used to be in the woods all you had to
watch for was junkies nodding off
getting caught with their ass in the bight
now its these Christly poets
scratching away behind every tree
trying to get you to repeat everything
gotta do your job and their job too
babysit the useless bastards
until the first plane goes out
Canada Council gives 'em ten thousand bucks
to write about what it's like
to be a workingman
tiny little book comes out
cost you half a day's pay to buy it
and here's all your own words
all phonied up so you sound like
some fucking Okie or something
everything's all ass-backwards
Jesus it makes me mad
if that guy ever shows up around here again
he'll have a real accident to write about

Bulldozer Joke

FIRST JOB

Two weeks ago he knew it was a snap
smart college boy like him deadheads like them
a week ago he'd given up all hope
today he thinks he has a chance
if he can only learn to beat
that sense of blindness backing up
steering one way in the mirror
Euc going the other way on the grade
but it's not to be today: first load
the fill gives   truck shifts
like the bottom falling out of the world
all he can do is clench with terror
only goes halfway over but road is blocked
seriousness of it mounts in his brain
as the other trucks roar up one by one
stop in a line   drivers gather
get out their thermos jugs ask nothing
mentally calculates lost earnings in the
thousands   someone mutters   looks up
foreman charging toward them
grimace under an orange hardhat
guts swimming around thinking
what a relief it would be to only be fired
hat goes by shouting orders comes back
"Alright get in there and be more careful!"
mouth works without words feet find the way
winchline tightens truck shudders wallows
slips back heaves up onto the road
like a walrus onto an ice floe
                              foreman gone

next day shovel cable breaks
trucks line up again coffee comes out
any excuse to take one away from the boss
the kid gets out his greasegun and rag
"Hey you, it's coffee time!"
"Aw, my truck needs greasing..."
keeps working
                    and that mistake
he must live much longer
                          to live down

CONNIE THE COOK

Connie the cook wanted to cut my hair.
She must have broached the subject twenty times
& finally one night I couldn't read
I remembered and went down.

She hacked away happily, reminded
by some announcement on Whitehorse radio
of a box lunch social when she was young
where her box went last to a drunk with 16¢.
"The others cheated," she says,
the hurt still in her voice.

You've got me looking like Moe of the 3 Stooges
I protest when she hands me the mirror
& she laughs till she's red as the fireweed
nodding and scratching at the window
"That's the way I used to do me brothers..."

But when I move toward the door
she steps in front of me & blurts,
"I saw you cuttin Keith's, Howard—
I was wondrin if you could trim me a bit
aroun the neck here...?"

and I say sure & wonder that
growth should still be a problem
on a head so grey & think
of her vanity that way—

it must have been a picture
the young catskinner in dirtstiff
pants and undershirt bent over this
prim little lady in uniform
white hands folded in lap
fumbling with the precious
snowy tassel of hair

"Huse t' do it meself
till me hand went bad," she says.
Her scalp shows pink
thru the fluff & sure enough
low on her neck I find grey
little brambles of growth

twisting out of the wrinkles.

BEFORE YOU KNOW IT

for my brother Don

On the spur of the moment I agreed to go
ended up in a plane a thousand miles away
stayed eight months in a forest of scrub
the size of France and occupied
by only the four people in camp

ten years later now I know those
ravens in that valley will be
pinned like sootspecks to the
light sky of my dreams forever
the horselike teeth of my
cardshark roommate flashing through
my lengthening nights

and bits of rutted country backroad
passed some time out of mind
chasing a job or some not even
beautiful woman I caught but
didn't talk to, just watched,
and then some again I did talk to
take to bed and live with for
unremarkable months, forgotten now.

How the random attachments of a morning
rise to possess the afternoon
and how the time of happenings

is soon over. If I'd known I was
stocking up my imagination
for the rest of my life
what I wouldn't have piled in.

LEVELING THE REVELSTOKE

Pink floppy ash and the glacier
floating in moonlight —
it is work now to remember
anything else, the great
defenceless cottonwoods swaying
week after week by the thousands
onto the ground, discs
of root popping up
twice the size of the cat
later pushed into huge piles
lined down the valley
like a convoy of supertankers —
the expropriation propaganda
called all Revelstoke Valley
"marginal farmland"
but the soil there was so
fluffy and deep if you
spun your tracks around twice
you'd bury the cat, hard
only where they'd had their
footpaths, like iron between
house and outhouse, only chipping
a bit at the passing of the cat.
The people we saw little other
sign of, only the softness left
on the wood of gatelatches
by their hard brown hands
axe-hewn barndoor timbers
polished black with use and the crust

on the cowplops still thin —
I remember racing Gary Spooner
D-8's clattering like a tank charge
down the main street of Arrowhead, B.C.
for the delicate single-spired church
that crumpled in a halo of fine,
fine white dust, not a doorpost
left standing by noon, the town scraped
from the map into a heap of
splintered boards that surprised
even us by its insignificance
as I was more than anything troubled
by the lack of resistance,
by the mechanical bloodlessness
of this defeat, the night
empty of offended spirits
and nothing to keep my own awake
but this feathery grey and pink ash
that exploded in a warm blizzard
from the big piles, wafting upward
over the valley like snow
freed of gravity, in one soft moment
transforming the wrecked valley floor
and our gleaming machines alike
into a blurred sad ghost
and at night, all hidden in the
mountains' blackness, only the glacier,
detached it seemed, by the moon,
floating coldly high overhead.

CIGARETTE MACHINE

Cartons so gloriously upholstered
I always hesitate to wreck them
    Peter Jacksons in
    aristocratic black and silver
    Exports iridescent
    emerald and ivory
(is the business so rich
it can afford to decorate
for inside men?)

I ponder
ways of harnessing waste glamour

handling the soft rich foil
you taste the money almost yours
    quarters pouring in
    all day and

    half for Imperial
    Tobacco/half
    for me

tearing boxes open, stuffing
the vertical magazines
keeping an eye
for sequence of colour
laying my money trap

only no trapper
was ever so sure
of his catch

what blessedness
    to stand against
the world

on the shoulders of tobacco giants

COFFEETIME AT KENO

was all idling diesels
and Keith
who had blue
holes in his teeth
and wished to be
rich
so he could live,
in aid of which he
cheated us at crib

    if you tramped a 988
    he told
    us, cold
    floorboarded it, it
    would fill this whole valley with smoke

he quit one
third way through

REALLY OUT IN THE BUSH

All day everyday back and forth
wearing down the South McQuestion
Valley to smoking bedrock
wearing out a new pair
of carbon steel corner bits every two days
and always wearing in the corner
of one eye or the other, our
motornoises sometimes wierdly harmonizing
old Jack   every twenty
minutes — every seven now
it's cold — stops
steps out on the track
starts digging
at his coveralls front
graphite-shiny from so much of it

> *five inches a fuckin underwear*
> *an only three inches a pecker*
> *jeeziz christ*

his kidneys gone from the booze
he guards like his gold
                    °
> *what a way*
> *to serve the Lord*

and
always no matter what

our respective positions or what
quarter the wind
keeping his back to me

for which I'm duly
grateful— 28 weeks
and a million acres of Yukon spruce
between us
and the next nearest eyes
that would matter
and privacy has never been
more dear.

BULLDOZER JOKE

It's been announced in the papers already
that the east side of this valley
will be flooded with its timber still standing
but Hydro is still threatening
to keep our holdback if so much
as a twig is left unburned
on the side we're clearing

so Spooner and I spend a whole hour
wallowing in the slough
mud working up through the tracks
wasting most of our time
trying to get unstuck
fishing for an old slime-pickled
hippopotamus of a river-log
that finally rears up splashing
and dripping from some hundred-year sleep,
balancing it between our blade
corners like a dinosaur couple
playing some party game
motors groaning diesel storm-clouds
"Now what?" Spooner hollers
just as the log twists
and dives back into the hole
and I follow it down in the
same motion, purposefully driving it down
too deep to be ever retrieved
or seen by the right-of-way inspector
in his chartered yellow Piper

Spooner grins hugely
thinking I couldn't tell you what
but I'm back in Vanguard Bay
eight years old scrambling eggs
for my old man and Robert LaRue
on a handlog show   haven't
washed my hands all week
shirtcuffs got that sewer smell again
and my nose drips a
great clear-jelly plop
right into the raw egg white
and Robert, when I look up
circles his hand excitedly
and whispers
                    "Stir! Stir! Stir!"

with that same grin.

DROWNING

Comes a point drowning reminds me of it
you get this eyes-unfocussed abstract look
refusing all further attempts at rescue —
woke up with pinching behind my ears
like icetongs caught there, slowly taking weight —
sheets like a bed of stinging nettles
daylight a dose of acid in my eyes.
Sleet that morning outside, flesh cringing
like a kicked dog eyelids flopping
up and down at each step
consciousness flickering at each breath
like a candle in a draught, confusion
roiling up at every turn of the head
like sediments in homebrew
and this would be the day we move the boxes.

It is not possible to describe how cold
an iron pinchbar can be to the hands
in mid-October in the Yukon in the sleet
except to note it for those who know.
Or the water, a week before freeze-up
running freely through your end-of-season
rubber boots. Everything hurt.
The sleet burnt hot on the tops of my ears.
Sand on the shovel handle cut into my skin
but there was no longer enough of me
left to wipe it off, or the rain
on my glasses making vision
a sickly hallucination. Pants stuck steaming

to one warm spot of thigh I'd lost
the will to move it off
boss hollering voice full of loathing,
everything hurts. I feel so pitiful
and the world is so relentless,
so harsh. Let me go, I make no pretence —
Twice, groping unspeakable depths
I pull myself out, put on a lame rush of action
slowing, the sweet numbness pooling inside
only the fear of letting go holding me back

cat slams one of the long wobbling boxes
unduly wild, someone cursing my sloth
pain like a coathanger wire
jammed up the core of my ulna
scorching a path to my toes
        FUCKINGHELLLLLL!
backing away, wound tucked in armpit
to a corner of the storm
staring
drowning
no one else impressed enough
to say for Chrissakes go sit in the truck

THE TRUCKDRIVER

It would be easy to talk about all the terrible accidents
we used to get into, but in all honesty I don't know
    how much worse it was
you'd see a man get killed once in a while just like you do now
I don't think anybody's been keeping score
God knows it shoulda been worse,
    when you compare what we did
sitting out in the open on a board seat
couple three-thousand-foot logs jiggling around
    behind your head
no bulkhead for protection wheel straining
    like a mad pig in your hands
trying to stay on those plank trestles with hard rubber tires
oh, a bit of mud or frost on those planks and it didn't matter
if you had brakes or not, looking down through a hundred feet
It was a different life, and it wasn't just the danger or the work
— it's hard to talk about it to anyone who wasn't there.
These big new Pacifics and Kenworths we have now,
    I don't know how
you could ever get into trouble, but they do.
When I first went hauling logs in the thirties
    we had three-ton Fords
old Bill Schnare had seized off farmers around the Fraser Valley
most of them had no doors or windows
    and we would bring single logs
with more scale in them than whole loads they get today
rattling and banging our way down Vedder Mountain,
    but nobody got hurt
on that job. We had those haywire old trucks working so good

you couldn't imagine it being done any better.
You got so you could hear the truck.
You'd had the goddamn thing apart
    so many times you were aware
of every goddamn bearing and how it was turning.
You'd see a new grease spot on the ground in the morning
and think, 'that Christly packing's come out again'
and if you didn't strip it down right there
    at least you'd make sure
it didn't run dry of oil that day. If the brakes started to go
you'd sense the slight change in the pedal, or you'd have caught
the wet spot on the wheel and be looking for it.
You got where nothing was an accident; it's always
you missed something or let something go.
    You weren't on the job.
And if you did get in a jam you knew how to get out of it.
Say you lose your brakes — the cooling water plugs up
    and the brakes burn up.
A driver who isn't with it doesn't know what's happening until
he's freewheeling down the mountain and there's nothing to do
but jump and knock his brains out on a stump.
The seasoned driver would have spotted the steam
    starting to thin out
five, ten minutes earlier and had time to do something.
The green guy, even if he did catch that,
    would dynamite right there
and push his hot brakedrums all out of shape,
    or else go for the ditch
and end up putting the load through the cab and getting smeared.
The other guy starts looking for the right spot to go off
where the trailer will hang up before the truck
and within an hour he's back on the road hauling logs.

Even a little thing like a mud puddle. You'll see the one guy
go half off the road to miss a
        little puddle the size of a dinner plate
then your cowboy comes ploughing straight through it,
the cold splash breaks the red-hot drums, the truck runs away
and they tell his widow, 'oh, the brakes failed.'
Today of course, with the miracle alloys they have, you never
have to think about anything like that. These young fellows
wouldn't live to see lunchtime on one of our old jobs,
        but try to tell them.
It's not that they're made out of such inferior stuff it's just
that in today's world the worker is given so much less to do.
This is the real change I've seen:
        it used to be the tools we had
were so minimal the only way you could survive was
by putting a hell of a lot of yourself into the job.
Jobs took years to learn, but once you'd done it
you could write your own ticket.
It was possible to achieve a sort of greatness in that work.
Now the genius has all been put into the machines
and all that's required of the worker is a kind of dumb obedience.
There's been a loss of scale, of human scale
but if you try to talk about it
they just look at you like you were crazy.

SWAMPY WALLACE

No one knows how he got that name and everyone asks —
like him not to have a story thought up even now
after all these years. 'Gumboot Logger.' I remember
Dad just furious. He really did turn up in rubbers
the first week, wrestling twisty chokers on slimy new slash.
One time so excited making the guitar strumming motion
fanning his shirtfront, he sprayed his buttons
all over the cookhouse.
      And then the fabulous babble,
still undiminished at fifty, giggling, hiccupping,
everything mushed together with lots of lips tongue spit
outburst of words kneeslap frantic wavings portly hops,
his family translating for him like a baby.

Swampy the drunken idiot, 'one of the Whiskey Slough Wallaces —'
worst of a bad lot so it was thought,
married a girl from Kinkum, first boy in jail
by age 14 — stupidly savage — fishboat finally burned
like everyone said it would, of filth in the bilge —
Swampy in hospital a roaring jumping mummy —

What happened? So unexpectedly moving to the city
and now back in a near-new car, painting his house to rent
his wife now in college and talking of going on to an MA
in English, kids married and back with kids, a parliament of
babbling new Wallaces, Swampy telling me some hardly likely
story of the time my Dad chewed one peanut all day —
they fight about who's the biggest idiot and I
rent the house.

He tells me not to worry about the money,
maybe my printshop ain't getting anywhere now
but I'll make it someday, hee hee hee hahaha

THE FISHERMAN AND THE LOGGER

You can spot a fisherman anywhere.
There is a roll to his walk.
There is a mournful whine in his voice,
sharpened by years of complaining about bad catches.
There's a sadness, a slowness, as if
too deep knowledge of the darkness below life's surfaces
had taken the hurry out of him. A patience
born of waiting—waiting for weather and tide
waiting for the fish to appear.
No one learns more of waiting than the fisherman.

In the fisherman's eye is none of the animal spark
you find in the loggers' eyes, no scent
of male animal, twitching tail. Fishing
isn't so dumbly masculine a species of work as logging—
women take well to its slow but intricate rhythm.

The logger is up in the pub bothering the barmaids
and starting fights; the fisherman is down on the dock
sitting on a fish box jawing politics and mending gear.
The logger has a new tinsel shirt he will tell you
how outrageously he paid for, but it will
be on the floor, once used and ruined when he leaves.
The fisherman has on wool and tweeds bagged to his shape
and prefers to drink on the boat among his own.

In the eye of the fisherman is a diffuse deepness
like the cloudy gulf he lets his gear into,
and his mind. The logger's work is fast and dangerous;
he must keep his eyes wide open.

The fisherman works blind, feeling
his familiar but never-known world
with the sightless, superstitious part of the mind.

The logger is strong, like the land
but the fisherman is stronger

like the sea.

THE OYSTER SHUCKER

Jacketing books, a simple endless chore
overlooked by automation
I think of him — the image of him
rising again as the problem
of some refinement in my own
mechanics shows itself

belly to the tin trough
apron on and one hand gloved,
bothered by us watching
as the round sharp blade
draws his mind to the
awkward challenge
in his left hand

how to crack open this
thing ugly and dirty
as a newly dug stone
extricate the opalescent jelly
of the meat without
tearing the black
gelatinous lace of the mantle

how to do this rapidly
over and over
all day long
all year —
every time the seam
concealed a new way

the final problem only
to save his own mind
taken out in deftness —
"Some guys get
pretty fast — "
sizing up another barnacled
test of his existence

filling his pan with
casual magic, safe inside
the small, hard shell of his art

THE NEWSPAPERMAN

If he were elected President the newspaperman
would be called a babe-in-arms by his own kind
but he feels as he sits to begin
the working out of another story
that he has been writing since the earth was formed
vaguely remembers filing a story on it

Making his way each day across
the unchanging landscape of language
rivers to be routinely forded, cliffs
to be scaled always with the same
little kit of words
words thumbworn and threadbare
always miraculously new again
each time they're laid out
screwed together, hung from a limb

and swish, out over the fathomless chasm he swings
making the side opposite just barely
(he makes it more difficult for his own amusement)
the old spent words left scattered
like old shotgun shells as he passes
over the distant ridge and on down
to the Press Club for a couple doubles
maybe a couple more before
stepping out the door
into a night of dreams that lay lifeless and pale
under the weight of used-up words

POETRY EDITOR

Reading John's latest manuscript
lost in his dreams
I feel the pages I've read
and the pages I've not
to see how far I've got
I've had it three months
he comes in an hour
I will have to
skip a few —
I've dealt with these
fine minds, their
crepuscular gropings
for long enough now to know
it won't matter

one connection
and they will be
satisfied, two
and they will die for you

NEVER MARRY A WRITER

It went this far once,
like an English 40 paradox come to life
I was lying in bed in the middle of the night
with the woman I am daily faced
with the problem of loving
   hit by this tremendous
upwelling of warm billowing joyous
IMAGINATIVENESS
which immediately developed into
two poems and
another idea—
to make actual love and

I'm pleased to say I took that
latter more travelled path
fully knowing the poems
would be thus lost in the night
   (though only after realizing
the symbolic implications
of the situation) and
I did write this
          later

SEWAGE POEM

The filth
that is the first corollary
of all that is clean
and green and living

so neatly and completely extracted
taken care of
by efficient stainless steel
gleaming white porcelain
never even seen
year in and out
nothing
is so unexpected
as the stopped-up drain
like a nightmare puking
of repressed memory
there are last week's teabags
long forgotten tampax
black old shit moving
in slow hypnotic circles staring up
with bright yellow eyes of the
corn fed Sunday's guests
invading the bathtub
climbing out of the sinkdrain
onto clean dinnerplates
a fullscale rebellion of the sludge

anger wastes itself ridiculous against it
it outlasts the suicidal surrender of all caring

waiting on some far more
crass and dreadful level
driving one beyond extremity
finally to
roll up sleeves
and get out the coathanger

HAYWIRE

I'm walking to work at 10 a.m.
under my arm a
taken for granted black box
with tools — it was
my mother's, she
got it with her
wood carving set
it has racks for that
but my father got me
tools for Christmas
he always gets me tools
a couple handfuls, loose
but my mother seeing this —
it was her own fault in a way —
said you can't just give
someone a handful of tools
dumped the carving set
out on the floor, put
my tools in the box
there now
that makes it something
    So here I walk
in the late morning.
Her carving set lies scattered.

I whistle.

It is typical.

IN THESE DREAMS

The child
chirping imitation
imagination clear
as a mirror
on his own

Whatcha doin
Douglas
           aw nothing
puts on a drab mask
and myself
all day on the cat
thoughts flutter and swoop
each one cutting
cleaner
           sideslip
           & dive
guided by
wisdom from the sky
so close to perfect
as to
           pain the mind

till I move
to write or speak, then
like oil on water
blooming unearthly colour

from a close
angle, all is
olive drab —

in these dreams
what we seek is
not a beyond world
but an angle on this one
that admits
no getting back to

PICKIN DANDELIONS

Driving home from Mt. Currie there
all the flat bright green fields
cows reducing to pepper specks on 'em
every inch crowded with business—
sheep, cattle, dairy cows and the huge
ploughed fields of what I guess were
Pemberton spuds—this is on the white side
and then on the Indian side,
fences grey and fallen, steep roofed
log barns with shingles mostly blown off
by this same wind that peppers the pickup roof
with blown bits of the neighbourhood
and the fields better even than the whites'
cooler and damper, flashing at us mile
after mile orangey yellow dandelions
and it gets to me and I say to Mare
hey, jesus, maybe we should stop
and grab some dandelions for wine
but she sez, ah, I wanna get home
but the flashes, solid yellow roadside strips
and vast flat spaces with the gold dust
salted over it, solid here, shaded there
over the green, and finally she says
yeah maybe we should stop
so we drive down onto this one field
the truck floating off in a sea of shifting gold
not so bright right here, not so bright
as further on I say but Mare she says
it's one a them oppital allusions dodo

it just looks like that, you'll never
get to the thick spot so we bend to it
first nipping the heads off with our thumbnails
which is cute but not something you can do fast
Mare she holds the stem I see, and pulls
the head a Mt. Currie basket between us
going through patches logic getting shown up again
as it becomes unmistakeable some patches *are*
better than others our technique fast refining
under pressure of such simple rapid repetition
trying the kneeling position, no that ain't good,
discovering the staring-you-in-the-face easiest
way is best, just yank the heads and they break
neatly at the stemjoint on their own
filling my hands instead of reaching to the basket
a million times, then expanding on that idea,
filling my bellied out shirtfront pickpickpick
that sound exactly, that sharp—pickpickpick
now Mare gets her own bag and I with the courage
finally of my first sense go to where the optical
illusion was, find the dandelions almost
no room between 'em, sweep them in
early on having found you can pick seven new ones
in the time it takes you to retrieve one dropped
though that is what you start out doing
if you're a whiteman and every pick,
the gum on your hands gets thicker
the yellow glow on your arms gets brighter
and the dandelion gets more beautiful
in the Indian sun.

MY YOUNG BROTHER DON

The way my young brother Don
flips up a paper
is significant to me.
He's sitting in the good chair
by the stove, legs crossed
with one big boot towards our faces
and he takes the paper
on each side, firm,
and goes "crack"
straightens it and reads,
ignoring our conversation.
He used to be so gentle,
he was the baby,
but he has just come back
from working in the camps.
His voice is growly and loud
as he calls for more tea, he swears
in front of his mother and he
twists the wheel of his
compliant Ford between rough hands.
But still, it is home
he has come to.
It is his father
he rides around all day with
showing these new improvements to
and the first night he is left alone
in the big house
it is my door he comes to,
smiling awkwardly,
    without much
    to say.

BOBBY KENNEDY PLACES

Just by the kitchen sink there
is a place I always think
of Pete, not because I
ever saw him there or
he ever even was there
it is because once, reaching
into the fridge for the milk
I saw Pete in my mind there
in a way I'd never seen him
before but always have since.

And so in the garden there
is a corner an admirable
indefatigable buttercup grows,
every time I chop it out
I am given to think of my
fading ambition to write poems

The grass grows, the rains
renew the ground and my
passing is continually erased.
What remains to inhabit
these places? A construct
in spirit. "The mind puts
in place/like rocks simple markers..."
Or more mysteriously
springs occur in the mind's ground,
upwellings of unpredictable duration

one of the longest where I was
working when I heard Bobby
Kennedy was shot, a goldmine
in the Yukon so that now
whenever I either think of the
North or any of these things
that make me think of other things
I think of Bobby Kennedy.

It is only through the brain's
peculiarity, changing all to metaphor,
the world becomes a known place.
Things the local government is
doing now brings in an old neurosis—
I clench my right fist until it
locks in pain. This goes back to
Gordie Gough in highschool
but clear as that is to me
no one else will ever see it.

What can be seen are the deposits
of calcium now stiffening my fingers.
I think of medical students someday
looking at my bones, noting
this roughness with
dispassionate curiosity
all my places fallen mute.